IMAGES
of England

IMMINGHAM

AND THE

GREAT CENTRAL LEGACY

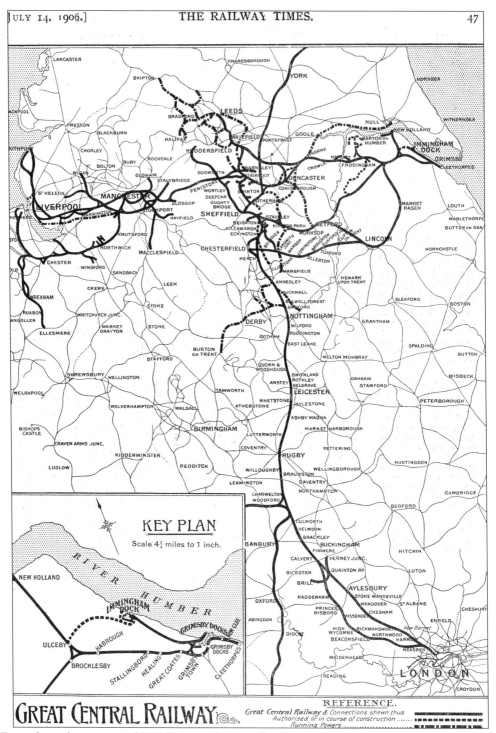

From the railway times of 14 July 1906 showing the Great Central Railway's main lines with local inset.

IMAGES
of England

IMMINGHAM

AND THE

GREAT CENTRAL LEGACY

Compiled by
Brian Mummery and Ian Butler

TEMPUS

First published 1999
Copyright © Brian Mummery and Ian Butler, 1999

Tempus Publishing Limited
The Mill, Brimscombe Port,
Stroud, Gloucestershire, GL5 2QG

ISBN 0 7524 1714 2

Typesetting and origination by
Tempus Publishing Limited
Printed in Great Britain by
Midway Clark Printing, Wiltshire

GCR class 8F 4-6-0 express goods engine *Immingham* built by Beyer Peacock in 1906. It was designed for fast goods and fish traffic but used on passenger work. This engine, No.1097, worked a special train to the ceremony of cutting the first sod for the Immingham dock.

Contents

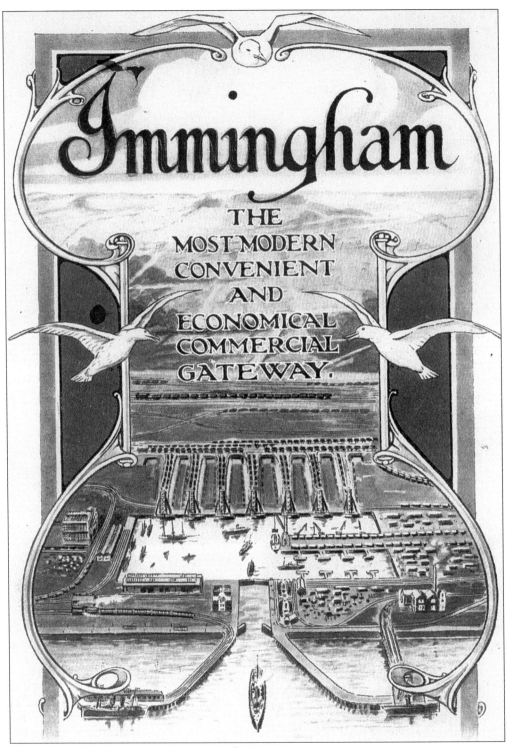

Great Central Railway promotion poster of 1912.

Introduction

For centuries, the sparsely populated marshland village of Immingham, seven miles to the north-west of Grimsby, had existed as a remote agricultural settlement, lying one mile inland from the south bank of the river Humber. In 1900, the nearest railway station was (and still is) two miles away, at Habrough.

In the first decade of the twentieth century, things began to change radically. The Great Central Railway, newly renamed from the Manchester, Sheffield and Lincolnshire Railway following the completion of its extension to London, announced its intention to build a new dock near the village to relieve congestion in the Grimsby dock estate.

Over several years, the village was to see the influx of a workforce of several thousand men, some with their families, to excavate the forty-five acre dock and develop the 1,000 acre estate.

Three railways were laid from Grimsby, Ulceby and Goxhill to access the new port. Seven hydraulic hoists were erected, capable of loading almost 5,000 tons of coal per hour into the holds of visiting ships, with 170 miles of sidings to accommodate the full and emptied wagons. A massive grain storage plant was also built and cranes were installed to load and discharge general cargoes, with transit sheds for their storage.

The entrance lock from the Humber was built to allow access to any ship which was able to pass through the Suez Canal, the gateway to the far eastern part of the British Empire. A large graving dock was excavated and a power station erected. Jetties projected into the river on each side of the lock entrance, the eastern jetty carrying a railway with passenger platform, the western a coal hoist for supplying fuel for ships' bunkers.

In addition to the three access railways, an electric powered light railway was laid alongside the line from Grimsby to carry the construction workers and, later, the dock workforce to and from Grimsby. Train services were also provided from Hull, via the Humber ferry and the line from Goxhill, and from Grimsby, via the main line to Habrough and through Ulceby. Both of these services terminated at the passenger station built to the west of the lockpit, adjacent to the graving dock.

At that time virtually all inland transport was by rail, and to service the large numbers of railway engines needed to move the traffic a thirteen-road engine shed was built, with an attendant dormitory for the use of visiting footplate crews.

Further afield, the increased traffic generated by the port forced the quadrupling of the railway tracks between Brocklesby and Wrawby junctions on the main line from Grimsby to the west and, even further afield, the construction of an avoiding line around Doncaster.

Although many of the workforce travelled in from Grimsby each day, a significant number came to live locally. During the construction period the village took on the appearance of a colonial frontier town with temporary corrugated iron buildings being erected as dwellings, stores and shops, before the appearance of more substantial buildings such as the County Hotel, the police station, the row of shops at Market Buildings and the surrounding terraced streets.

From the cutting of the first sod on 12 July 1906 by Lady Henderson, the wife of the Great Central's Chairman, Sir Alexander Henderson, it took six years of heavy work before the official opening of the dock by HM King George V on 22 July 1912. On this occasion the King bestowed a knighthood, on the spot, on Sam Fay, the Great Central's manager and prime mover of the completed development.

Two years after the opening, the country was at war with Germany. The Royal Navy took full advantage of the port facilities and used the port as a base for submarines and fast patrol boats. They also set up a seaplane station on the Humber bank at nearby North Killingholme, reached from the dock's Goxhill rail branch. The seaplane station was temporarily taken over by the US Navy following their entry into the war.

Twenty-five years later the country was again at war with Germany. The dock was once more taken into military use: a destroyer squadron commanded by Lord Mountbatten was based there and the RAF established an air/sea rescue launch base within the dock.

Between the wars, the port never had the opportunity to realize its true potential due to the decline in international trade. For several years, regular summertime cruises to the Norwegian Coast were operated from the eastern, rail-connected jetty – the 'Midnight Sun Cruises' – using passenger liners of 14,000 to 23,000 tons and attracting passengers nationwide.

The port really came into its own following the Second World War, with heavy industrial expansion taking place within and around the dock area to the point where the local newspaper recently acclaimed it to be the UK's busiest port. The small marshland village has grown into a township of 13,000 people.

The Great Central Railway passed into history in 1923 when it was absorbed into the London & North Eastern Railway, but its global influence continues to expand. Surely a Great Central legacy!

A striking shot of class 8F No.1100 at the head of a mixed train, c.1921.

One
The Rural Village

THATCHED COTTAGE & LANE, IMMINGHAM.

Immingham. The Saxon village changed little until the construction of the dock that suddenly brought the village into the twentieth century.

This view of Church Lane shows the mud and stud cottage occupied by the Collingwood family. Later buildings, erected at the turn of the century, are also visible.

Another view of the Collingwood's cottage taken around 1890.

Local wheelwright and joiner Mr Rands and his workmen, *c.*1904.

George Penny Nicholson, Immingham's first postman, outside the thatched post office, *c.*1900

A nineteenth-century map showing the haven where the dock would eventually be built.

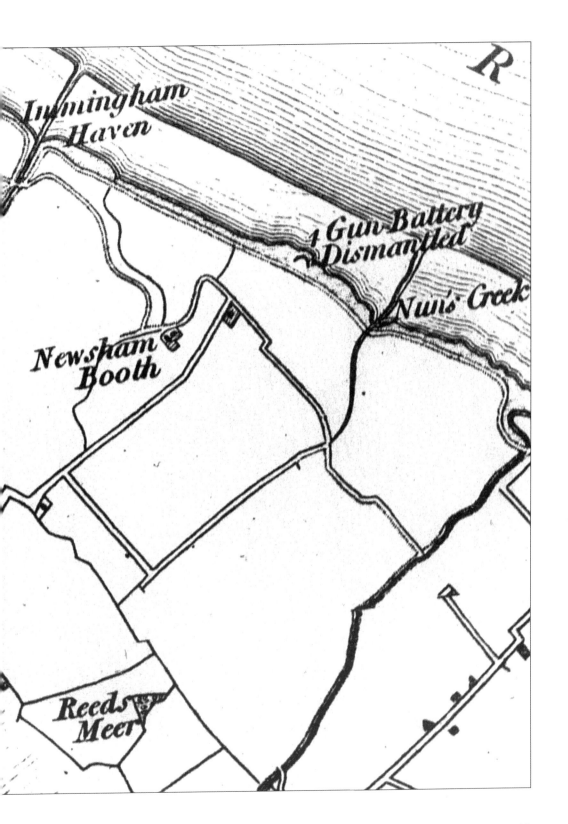

Immingham Haven

4 Gun Battery Dismantled

Nun's Creek

Newsham Booth

Reeds Meer

R

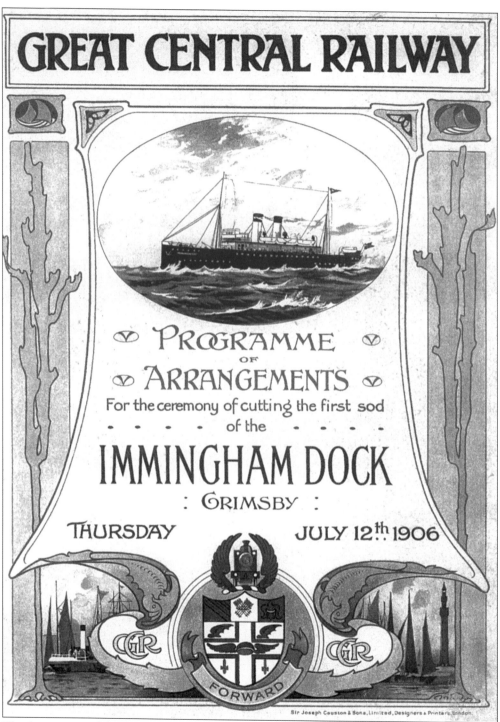

GREAT CENTRAL RAILWAY

❧ PROGRAMME ☙
OF
❧ ARRANGEMENTS ☙
For the ceremony of cutting the first sod
· · · · · of the · · · ·

IMMINGHAM DOCK
: GRIMSBY :

THURSDAY   JULY 12th 1906

FORWARD

Sir Joseph Causton & Sons, Limited, Designers & Printers, London.

The front cover of the official programme for the sod-cutting ceremony. The original programme is displayed in the Immingham Museum.

Two
A Time Of Change – A New Dock Is Born

The first bore is sunk, 1906.

Lady Henderson performs the ceremony of cutting the first sod for the new dock. Prominent board members of the Great Central Railway, together with church and local dignitaries, are in attendance. The spade lying on the ground is the actual spade used to loosen the sod before the ceremony. It is now displayed in Immingham Museum.

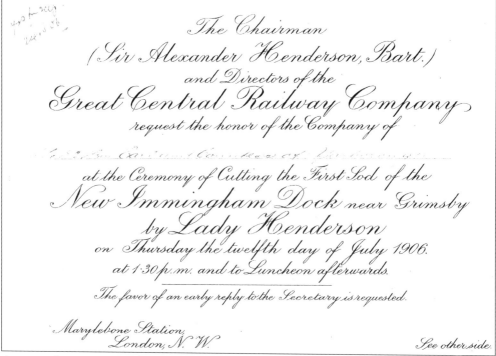

The Chairman
(Sir Alexander Henderson, Bart.)
and Directors of the
Great Central Railway Company
request the honor of the Company of

at the Ceremony of Cutting the First Sod of the
New Immingham Dock near Grimsby
by Lady Henderson
on Thursday the twelfth day of July 1906.
at 1·30 p.m. and to Luncheon afterwards.

The favor of an early reply to the Secretary is requested.

Marylebone Station,
London, N.W.   *See other side.*

A personal invitation to the Earl and Countess of Yarborough for the sod-cutting ceremony. Lord Yarborough was a director of the railway.

THE GREAT CENTRAL RAILWAY COMPANY'S NEW IMMINGHAM DOCK.

On Thursday, Lady Henderson, wife of Sir Alexander Henderson, Chairman of the Great Central Railway, cut the first sod of the Company's new Immingham Dock. For some time proposals have been made for a deep water dock on the Grimsby side of the Humber, and as early as 1873 a scheme was prepared. It was not until 1901, however, that the first Humber Commercial Railway and Dock Act authorising the construction of such a dock adjoining the existing docks at Grimsby was passed. In response to representations made by important Grimsby interests the Company agreed to facilitate in every way an enterprise for a new dock if promoted independently by Grimsby people with the full support of Grimsby, and to take a lease of any such dock sanctioned, and if proved to be satisfactory from an engineering point of view. The Humber Commercial Dock Company was consequently formed, and the Act of 1901 obtained.

The idea of transferring the dock from Grimsby to Immingham was regarded at first with hostility at Grimsby, but after the Corporation and other Grimsby authorities had made inquiries for themselves, they became strong advocates of the Immingham scheme, which was introduced into Parliament in 1903 by the same parties who obtained the first Act, and was heartily supported by every person of importance connected with the south side of the Humber, though some opposition came from Hull, mainly on the question of possible interference with the Humber channel.

The Committee of the House of Commons passed the preamble of the bill in 1903, subject to a clause throwing upon the Great Central Company the obligation of making good any defect which might thereafter occur in the channels of the Humber, and which an expert appointed by the Board of Trade might decide to be attributable to the new dock. Under these circumstances it was decided to withdraw the bill, but the Great Central Railway Company was strongly pressed to give its support to a renewal of the scheme in another session of Parliament. The proposal was accordingly again submitted to Parliament in 1904, the Board of Trade having previously had a report made on the points raised by the Hull authorities, and the Humber Commercial Railway and Dock Act was passed for the dock now in course of construction.

Photo by]   [Langfier, London.

LADY HENDERSON,

who, on Thursday, cut the first sod of the Immingham Dock.

Extract from *The Railway News* of 14 July 1906 announcing the commencement of work on the dock, with a photograph of Lady Henderson.

Mr Hollowday, great grandson of Robert Hollowday, works manager for the dock's builders, shows off the original silver mounted wheelbarrow and spade presented to Lady Henderson at the sod-cutting ceremony in 1906. The photograph was taken in 1987 at the seventy-fifth anniversary celebration of the opening of the dock.

Dignitaries arrived for the sod-cutting ceremony on 12 July 1906 in a special train. Here tank engine *Prescot* pulls what is thought to be the Great Central's director's saloon.

The Hollowday family. Robert Hollowday was manager and agent for the firm of Price, Wills and Reeves, the main contractors in the building of the new dock at Immingham for the Great Central Railway. Robert, two of his brothers and three of his elder sons had been engaged on dock building for the company for several years. Immingham was to be his last contract in a long career which included work in Cyprus, India, Singapore and Burma. He died in 1924 aged seventy-five. The photograph, taken in 1910, shows Robert with his six sons, five of whom were engaged in dock construction.

More ceremony guests arriving in somewhat basic fashion!

A posed photograph of navvies from the construction period.

Early construction work on the dock basin.

Steam power in use on the construction.

Many small tank locos were used. This one is working spoil from the dock.

The lock gates under construction.

A steam shovel working on what would become the dock bottom.

Pile driving in the Humber for the eastern and western jetties.

A general view of dock construction in progress.

The power station takes shape.

Construction work on the south quay wall.

Erection of coal hoists.

A superb view of the outer and middle lock gates nearing completion.

The dock offices are built.

Beaufort is believed to be the first locomotive to work in the dock bottom. The driver John Thomas is about to board.

A steam-driven bucket excavator working in the dock.

High level serving road No.1 under construction. The serving roads were for delivering the loaded coal wagons to the dockside hoists.

Miles of railway lines were needed for the dock. Here a gang of platelayers take a rest.

FIRST VESSEL TO ENTER IMMINGHAM DOCK.

The first ship to enter the new dock prior to the official opening, the SS *Max*, dressed overall for the occasion.

Great Central Railway,
General Manager's Office,
Marylebone Station,
London, N.W.

TELEGRAMS:-
"FAY
MARYLEBONE STATION,
LONDON."

Dear Sir,

    The sustained shipping activity on the Humber during the last few years has taxed the capacity of the existing Docks to the utmost, and to meet the demand for better and more up-to-date facilities, my Company has been engaged in the construction of a new Deep Water Dock at Immingham, about six miles above Grimsby.

    This Dock will be unquestionably the deepest on the East Coast, and is reached by a well buoyed and lighted deep-water channel running in a straight line direct from the North Sea, which, combined with the great depth of water on the sill, affords vessels of even the largest size and deepest draft the exceptional advantage of being able to enter or leave dock at any state of the tide.

    By the same post a copy of the "Transit Annual" of 1911 is being sent you, and on pages 31 to 40 will be found further details of the undertaking.

    Any shipping which you may now or in the future be able to direct to this Dock will, I feel sure, be dealt with entirely to your satisfaction.

    Should you desire any further information respecting facilities or charges, please communicate with the Portmaster, Mr. F. M. Barwick, Immingham Department, Grimsby Docks.

    CARGO AND BUNKER COAL IS NOW BEING SHIPPED AT THE WESTERN JETTY AND THE DOCK ITSELF WILL BE OPEN FOR BUSINESS IN OCTOBER NEXT.

        Yours faithfully,

        Sam Fay

A letter from the GCR signed by Sam Fay, with the intent of generating more shipping custom.

Above, below and following page: Some of the publicity postcards published before the opening.

GREAT CENTRAL RAILWAY.

OPENING OF

IMMINGHAM DOCK

BY

HIS MAJESTY THE KING,

Accompanied by HER MAJESTY THE QUEEN.

MONDAY, JULY 22nd, 1912.

The cover of the official programme for the opening of the dock by HM King George V on Monday 22 July 1912.

Three
The Grand Opening

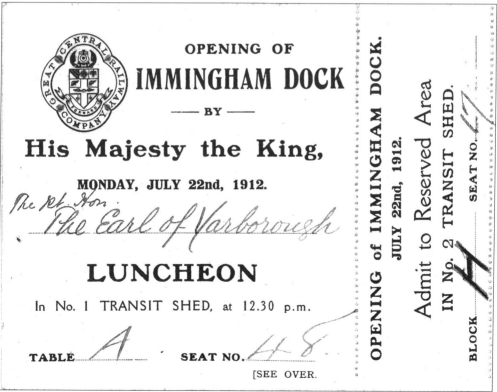

OPENING of IMMINGHAM DOCK.

JULY 22nd, 1912.

Admit to Reserved Area

IN No. 2 TRANSIT SHED.

SEAT NO.

BLOCK

OPENING OF

IMMINGHAM DOCK

—— BY ——

His Majesty the King,

MONDAY, JULY 22nd, 1912.

The Rt. Hon.

The Earl of Yarborough

LUNCHEON

In No. 1 TRANSIT SHED, at 12.30 p.m.

TABLE _____ · SEAT NO. _____

[SEE OVER.

The pass issued to the Earl of Yarborough when attending the royal opening.

Above and below: The Paddle Steamer *Killingholme* passes through the lock carrying the royal party.

The *Killllingholme* approaches its berth. HM Queen Mary is clearly visible in white to the left of the upper deck.

Another photograph of the *Killingholme* approaching its berth. At the time she was a Humber ferry and was owned by the GCR.

The Queen disembarks.

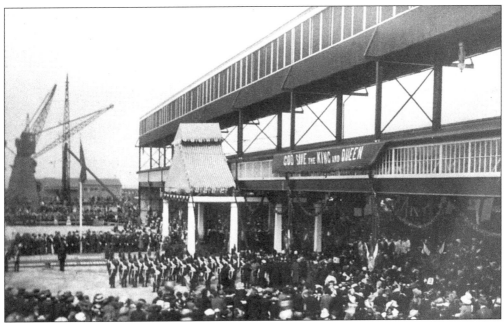

Above and below: Views of the guests, bands, paraded troops and general public at the opening ceremony.

Miss Joyce Barwick – daughter of the portmaster – with the bouquet she presented to the Queen.

An official guest pass.

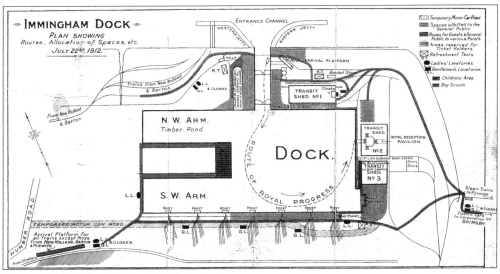

A map published with the official invitations.

The front cover of the brochure issued with the official invitation. The original is displayed in

FFICIAL OPENING
OF
MINGHAM DOCK
BY
MAJESTY THE KING
July 22nd 1912

Immingham Museum.

TRAIN ARRANGEMENTS

THE following Special Trains will be run for the convenience of Guests invited to the Ceremony :—

LONDON (Marylebone)	...	...	...	...	...	depart	8.15 a.m.
LEICESTER (Central)	...	...	...	...	...	,,	10.20 ,,
NOTTINGHAM (Victoria)	...	...	...	...	...	,,	10.47 ,,
IMMINGHAM	...	...	...	...	...	arrive	1.20 p.m.

Breakfast will be served between London and Leicester

IMMINGHAM	...	...	...	...	...	depart	4.5 p.m.
NOTTINGHAM (Victoria)	...	...	...	...	...	arrive	6.43 ,,
LEICESTER (Central)	...	...	...	...	...	,,	7.10 ,,
MARYLEBONE	...	...	...	...	...	,,	9.15 ,,

Dinner will be served after leaving Leicester

MANCHESTER (London Road)	...	...	...	...	...	depart	9.30 a.m.
MOTTRAM	...	...	...	...	...	,,	9.51 ,,
PENISTONE	...	...	...	...	...	,,	10.18 ,,
SHEFFIELD (Victoria)	...	...	...	...	...	,,	10.40 ,,
ROTHERHAM	...	...	...	...	...	,,	10.51 ,,
DONCASTER	...	...	...	...	...	,,	11.16 ,,
IMMINGHAM	...	...	...	...	...	arrive	1.4 p.m.

IMMINGHAM	...	...	...	...	...	depart	4.15 p.m.
DONCASTER	...	...	...	...	...	arrive	6.7 ,,
ROTHERHAM	...	...	...	...	...	,,	6.29 ,,
SHEFFIELD (Victoria)	...	...	...	...	...	,,	6.40 ,,
PENISTONE	...	...	...	...	...	,,	7.7 ,,
MOTTRAM	...	...	...	...	...	,,	7.35 ,,
MANCHESTER (London Road)	...	...	...	...	...	,,	7.55 ,,

CHESTERFIELD (G.C.)	...	...	...	...	...	depart	9.35 a.m.
STAVELEY TOWN	...	...	...	...	...	,,	9.48 ,,
WORKSOP	...	...	...	...	...	,,	10.10 ,,
RETFORD	...	...	...	...	...	,,	10.24 ,,
LINCOLN	...	...	...	...	...	,,	10.55 ,,
BROCKLESBY	...	...	...	...	...	,,	11.54 ,,
IMMINGHAM	...	...	...	...	...	arrive	12.46 p.m.

IMMINGHAM	...	...	...	...	...	depart	4.25 p.m.
BROCKLESBY	...	...	...	...	...	arrive	5.17 ,,
LINCOLN	...	...	...	...	...	,,	6.15 ,,
RETFORD	...	...	...	...	...	,,	6.46 ,,
WORKSOP	...	...	...	...	...	,,	7.1 ,,
STAVELEY TOWN	...	...	...	...	...	,,	7.26 ,,
CHESTERFIELD (G.C.)	...	...	...	...	...	,,	7.38 ,,

CLEETHORPES	...	...	...	...	...	depart	12.15 p.m.
GRIMSBY DOCKS	...	...	...	...	...	,,	12.25 ,,
GRIMSBY TOWN	...	...	...	...	...	,,	12.33 ,,
IMMINGHAM	...	...	...	...	...	arrive	1.25 ,,

IMMINGHAM	...	...	...	...	...	depart	4.35 p.m.
GRIMSBY TOWN	...	...	...	...	...	arrive	5.27 ,,
GRIMSBY DOCKS	...	...	...	...	...	,,	5.35 ,,
CLEETHORPES	...	...	...	...	...	,,	5.45 ,,

NOTE.—In case any of the Guests travel by ordinary trains it will be necessary to arrive at Grimsby Town Station in time to join the Special Train leaving there at 12.33 p.m. for Immingham.

GCR instruction regarding special train arrangements.

The cover of the programme for the event.

Great Central Railway.

OPENING

OF THE

NEW DOCK AT IMMINGHAI

BY

HIS MAJESTY THE KING,

ACCOMPANIED BY HER MAJESTY THE QUEE

On MONDAY, 22nd JULY, 1912.

Programme.

A group of officials on the steps of the dock office. Sam Fay, with a beard, is prominent at the front centre.

Royal train drawn by Atlantic compound No.364 *Lady Henderson*.

Security instructions for the ceremony.

The King shakes the hand of a dock worker, watched by the Queen. The officer to the right of Her Majesty is Herbert Plumer, soon to become a commander in the First World War, not a later well-known German!

GREAT CENTRAL RAILWAY.

INSTRUCTIONS

To Station Masters, Inspectors, Engine Drivers, Guards, Platelayers, Signalmen and others concerned.

JOURNEY

OF

THEIR MAJESTIES

THE

KING and QUEEN and SUITE

FROM

KING'S CROSS

TO

IMMINGHAM DOCK

AND BACK,

On MONDAY, 22nd JULY, 1912.

NOTE.— These instructions must be kept strictly private, and must only be communicated to those persons in the service of the Company, who, in the discharge of their duty, require to know and act upon them; and those persons must not give any information whatever to anyone respecting the hours or other arrangements set forth in these instructions.

The cover to the instruction booklet issued to GCR staff involved in the royal journey.

Great Central Railway,

Marine Superintendent's Office.

M.1583.   Grimsby Docks

24th. July, 1912.

Dear Sir,

Opening Ceremony at Immingham Dock.

I am sorry I had not an opportunity of thanking you personally on Monday last, for the excellent manner in which you navigated the p.s. "Killingholme" with T.M. the King and Queen on board. I appreciate very much the assistance which you gave me throughout the whole of the proceedings and shall be glad if you will convey my best thanks to the crew for the helpful manner in which they discharged their duties.

Yours truly,

PRIVATE.

Captain Rulling,

Hull Ferryboats.

A letter of appreciation to the master of the Paddle Steamer *Killingholme* for his efforts at the opening.

Four
The Village Changes

A postcard showing Chapel Lane, now Pelham Road, c.1910. A modern garage now stands on the site occupied by the building on the right, which was the first chapel in Immingham, built prior to the expansion period.

Above, below and following page: Small temporary shops erected to serve the increased population give the village a frontier town look.

HUMBERVILLE
IMMINGHAM 7.

53

As the village grew, permanent buildings replaced the earlier temporary structures. This photograph shows the shops at Market Buildings.

The County Hotel and the police station.

Waterworks Street, with police houses on left and the water tower visible in the background.

Large family houses in Pelham Road.

Terraced houses in Spring Street. Note the unmade roads and the water tower in the background.

Kings Road.

Humberville Road.

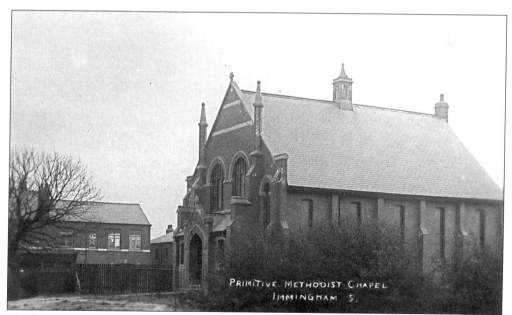

The Primitive Methodist Chapel in Pelham Road that opened in 1910.

Immingham's first taxi, 1910, with Mr J. Bellamy at the wheel.

The local grocer, Mr Cook, and his assistant, on the left. They were making deliveries with his model T Ford.

The Immingham Queen omnibus.

Driver George Stamp stands at the door of one of the other buses.

These corrugated bungalows in Pelham Road were built for the engineers working on the dock construction. Some survive to this day. Note the children playing in the unmade road, the main road through the village.

Five
The Clickety – The Immingham Trams

The road to Immingham from Grimsby was just a rough track and it was then necessary to provide transport for the workforce at the new dock and the loco depot. In order to do that, the GCR built a unique tramway system from Grimsby to Immingham Dock. The electric powered system, laid alongside the connecting railway from Grimsby, ran across the riverside marshes to Pyewipe before taking to the borough streets along Gilbey Road and Corporation Road to a terminus at Corporation Bridge. Cars, specially built for the system by Brush of Loughborough, came into use in 1912, the power being provided from the dock power station by overhead wires. Later additions and replacements to the fleet were purchased from Newcastle and Gateshead Corporations upon the closure of their tramways. This photograph shows one of the original cars when new in 1912. The car and its crew proudly display their GCR livery.

Great Central.

GRIMSBY AND IMMINGHAM
ELECTRIC RAILWAY.

TIME TABLE OF CARS.
WEEK-DAYS.

GRIMSBY (Corporation Bridge) depart—

a.m.	a.m.	p.m.
A 5 15	10 20	C 4 20
A 5 17	10 40	C 4 40
A 5 20	11 0	C 5 0
A 5 25	11 20	C 5 20
A 5 30	11 40	C 5 40
A 5 40	noon	C 6 0
A 6 0	12 0	C 6 20
A 6 20	p.m.	C 6 40
A 6 40	12 20	C 7 0
A 7 0	12 40	C 7 20
A 7 20	1 0	C 7 40
A 7 40	1 20	C 8 0
A 8 0	1 40	8 20
A 8 20	2 0	8 40
A 8 30	2 0	9 0
A 8 40	2 40	9 20
A 9 0	3 0	9 40
9 20	3 20	10 0
9 40	3 40	10 40
10 0	C 4 0	11 0
		11 20

IMMINGHAM DOCK depart—

a.m.	p.m.	p.m.
B12 20 M.X.	12 5 S.O.	B 5 20
D 6 0	12 20	B 5 30
D 6 20	12 30 S.O.	B 5 40
D 6 40	12 40	B 6 0
D 7 0	1 0	B 6 20
D 7 20	1 10 S.O.	B 6 40
D 7 40	1 20	B 7 0
D 8 0	1 40	B 7 20
8 20	2 0	B 7 40
8 40	2 20	B 8 0
9 0	2 40	B 8 20
9 20	3 0	B 8 40
9 40	3 20	B 9 0
10 0	3 40	B 9 20
10 20	B 4 0	B 9 40
10 40	B 4 20	B10 0
11 0	B 4 40	B10 20
11 20	B 5 0	B10 40
11 40	B 5 5 S.X.	B11 20
noon	B 5 10 S.X.	
12 0		

SUNDAYS.

GRIMSBY (Corporation Bridge) depart—

a.m.	p.m.	p.m.
6 0	1 0	6 20
8 0	1 40	7 0
9 0	2 20	7 40
9 40	3 0	8 20
10 20	3 40	9 0
11 0	4 20	9 40
11 40	5 0	10 40
p.m.	5 40	11 50
12 20		

IMMINGHAM DOCK depart—

a.m.	p.m.	p.m.
12 20	12 20	5 40
7 0	1 0	6 20
9 0	1 40	7 0
9 40	2 20	7 40
10 20	3 0	8 20
11 0	3 40	9 0
11 40	4 20	9 40
	5 0	11 15

S.O. Saturdays only.   S.X. Saturdays excepted.   M.X. Mondays excepted.

The Cars stop at the following places :—

YARBORO' STREET.   **CLEVELAND BRIDGE.**
STORTFORD STREET.   **IMMINGHAM TOWN.**

and by request at JACKSON STREET, BOULEVARD RECREATION GROUND, GREAT COATES LEVEL CROSSING and MARSH ROAD LEVEL CROSSING.

FARES.

Grimsby (Corporation Bridge) and Cleveland Bridge	... ...	1d.
,, ,, and Great Coates Level Crossing	... ...	2d.
,, ,, and Marsh Road Level Crossing	... ...	4d.
,, ,, and Immingham Town	... ...	5d.
,, ,, and Immingham Dock	... ...	6d.
Cleveland Bridge and Great Coates Level Crossing	... ...	1d.
,, and Marsh Road Level Crossing	... ...	3d.
,, and Immingham Town	... ...	4d.
,, and Immingham Dock	... ...	5d.
Great Coates Level Crossing and Marsh Road Level Crossing	... ...	2d.
,, ,, and Immingham Town	... ...	4d.
,, ,, and Immingham Dock	... ...	5d.
Marsh Road Level Crossing and Immingham Town	... ...	2d.
,, ,, and Immingham Dock	... ...	3d.
Immingham Town and Immingham Dock	... ...	2d

WORKMEN'S DAILY RETURN TICKETS, Grimsby to Immingham Dock ... ... **3d.**
Are issued to bona-fide Workmen by Cars marked "A" available to return by Cars marked "B," and by Cars marked "C" available to return by Cars marked "D."
On Saturdays only, Workmen's Daily Return Tickets are available to return by any Car after 12 noon.

Marylebone Station,
London, N.W., June 12th, 1914.
50/5,000—15-6-14.   G. N. G.

SAM FAY,
General Manager.

A timetable and fare schedule for June 1914.

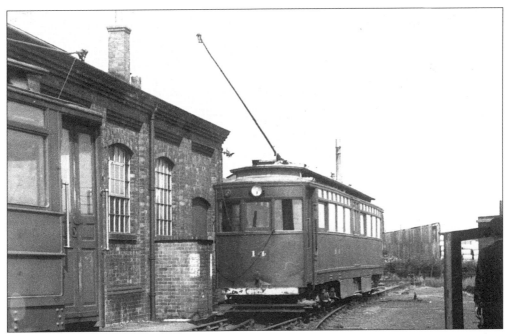

Car No.14 at the Pyewipe maintenance depot in LNER days. This car is now preserved in working order at the Crich Tramway Museum.

Brand new GCR car No.2 stands outside the Pyewipe depot.

CHEAP RETURN TICKETS

will be issued

EVERY DAY

UNTIL FURTHER NOTICE

BETWEEN

GRIMSBY and IMMINGHAM

(Corporation Bridge)   (Dock)

IN BOTH DIRECTIONS,

ALSO FROM AND TO ANY
INTERMEDIATE POINT.

Fare–1/-

AVAILABILITY:

Outward - - By any car after 9·0 a.m.

Return - - By any car on day of issue

IMMINGHAM DOCK. — An attractive outing is afforded by a Day Trip to Immingham Dock. Electric Cars leave Grimsby Corporation Bridge at short intervals and proceed along the "Humber" bank to the Dock.

Tickets and Bills of the above can be obtained any time in advance.

For further information apply to the District Manager, Lincoln, or the Passenger Manager, Liverpool Street Station, London, E.C 2.

London, December 1929.

5,000

No. 1983

An LNER promotional handbill from 1929 offering cheap return tickets on the trams.

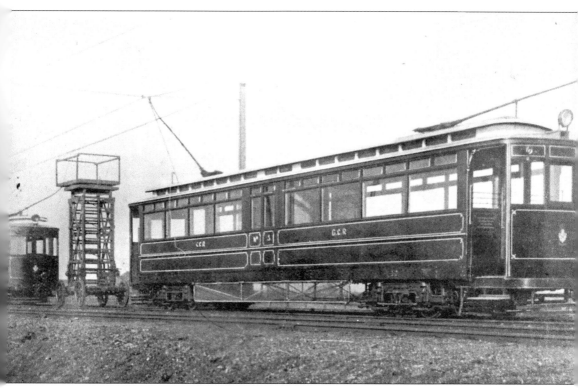

GCR car No.3 in prime condition. The overhead inspection trolley stands to its left.

'In the sticks'. A procession of cars crosses the marshes. Up to six cars were required at shift changeover times. Ex-Newcastle car No.8 leads the field.

On reaching Kings Road, Immingham, reversal was necessary to proceed to the terminus near the lockpit. The junction trackwork can be clearly seen in this view. Some of the large concrete wire supports still stand.

The crew of car No.11 take a break at Kings Road.

Car No.16 makes its way along the Corporation Road street section in LNER days.

The last tram, 1 July 1961, seen near the Pyewipe depot. Other cars from the fleet are lined up, ready for disposal, in the background.

A group of local factory workers pose in front of the decorated last tram. Worn out after forty-nine years of heavy and continuous service, the electric railway finally closed in 1961. The Grimsby Street section had already been closed five years earlier when the Pyewipe depot became the terminus.

Six

Great (Central)
Expectations

The GCR had high hopes for the prosperity of its new venture, as can be seen from this 1912 publicity poster.

An inter-war view matches the optimism of the previous photograph.

The grain trade was to feature strongly in the prosperity of the port. This huge concrete granary was a prominent feature on the dockside.

GRAIN WAREHOUSE, IMMINGHAM.

Another view of the granary. The quay on the left was the scene of the official opening ceremony.

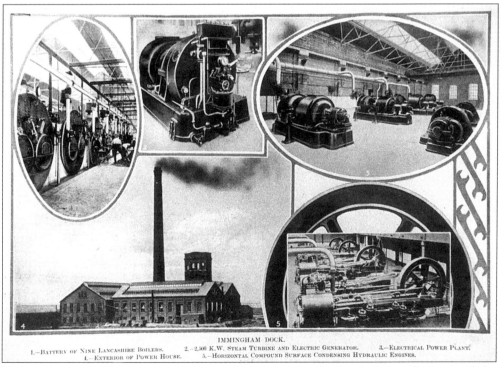

IMMINGHAM DOCK.
1.—BATTERY OF NINE LANCASHIRE BOILERS.   2.—2,500 K.W. STEAM TURBINE AND ELECTRIC GENERATOR.   3.—ELECTRICAL POWER PLANT.
4.—EXTERIOR OF POWER HOUSE.   5.—HORIZONTAL COMPOUND SURFACE CONDENSING HYDRAULIC ENGINES.

High technology! The power station provided electricity for the dock installations and the electric trams.

The completed dock offices.

Coaling. The stark silhouettes of the hoists stand out against the sky.

Coaling. An unknown ship awaiting its cargo.

Coaling – the reality!

BIRDS EYE VIEW, IMMINGHAM

Looking across the dock from the coal hoists towards the lockpit. The large ship beyond the

cranes is berthed alongside the dry dock and may be under repair.

Full coal wagons lined up ready for loading into the waiting ship.

A view of the coal hoists in operation. The quality of the photograph doesn't detract from its interest.

This rare photograph shows a sailing ship discharging wool bales onto the Immingham quayside.

295 WESTERN JETTY, IMMINGHAM DOCK.

The western jetty, projecting into the river, was built for the purpose of bunkering coal fired ships (i.e. replenishing the ship's fuel stock).

A Polish ship takes on bunker coal. This later shot shows the addition of railway track on the wooden jetty.

The premises of C.W. Hewson, ship's chandler and alderman of the Borough of Grimsby, with his fleet of delivery lorries standing alongside. Road transport began to invade the railway monopoly after the First World War, when the government sold off large numbers of war surplus lorries at knock-down prices. Hewson's fleet appears to be largely made up of such vehicles. The premises were later destroyed in a fire.

The fleet modernizes. An Albion lorry with trailer. This is believed to be a publicity photograph.

Driver Mr J. Bellamy poses in front of two of Hewson's fleet. No doubt the extra advertising revenue from *Bisto* would help the firm's profitability!

A superb shot of an AEC eight-wheeler from Hewson's fleet. The less than perfect condition and attached trade plates may suggest it having been sold.

SS *Immingham*, a further indication of the GCR's pride in their new port. This triple screw addition to the company's fleet was built by Swan Hunter and launched in 1906 for the near continental trade.

A later photograph of the same ship. The *Immingham* was found to be overpowered and was converted to single screw propulsion, with one funnel only, in 1911.

Another of the company's ships, the SS *Dewsbury*, was the first vessel to use the bunkering facility on the western jetty on its maiden voyage in April 1910, two years before the completion of the dock.

A group of GCR sailors. Note the bare feet!

Ship's officers from the GCR fleet. Judging by the medals, this is possibly a wartime or post-First World War photograph

The port goes to war! A flotilla of torpedo boats moored in the dock basin.

TORPEDO BOATS
IMMINGHAM DOCK

A more detailed view of the torpedo boats.

A row of submarines in dock.

Loading the tin fishes! A torpedo is taken aboard one of the submarines.

Kaiser beware! The navy is about to leave port.

The return of the hunter. Was it a success? A submarine approaches the lock.

Jack Cornwell VC. Sixteen-year-old boy seaman first class John Travers Cornwell was serving aboard the cruiser HMS *Chester* at the battle of Jutland on 31 May 1916. While he was at his post as message relayer for the forward gun turret, three enemy shells hit the turret killing all the other gun crew. Cornwell, although severely wounded, remained at his post, awaiting relief. He was landed at Immingham the following day, and transferred to hospital in Grimsby, where he died on 2 June 1916. He remains the youngest holder of the Victoria Cross.

The Midnight Sun Cruises. In the 1920s and 1930s, Immingham was used as a starting point for cruises to the Norwegian fjords during the summer months. Trains arrived on the eastern jetty and passengers simply walked the few yards to the waiting ship's gangway.

Empress of Australia, formerly *Tirpitz*, before seizure as war reparations. This was one of the largest of the liners using Immingham, with a weight of about 21,000 tons.

SS *Avon* lying off Immingham. A crowd of sightseers on the Humber Paddle Steamer are obviously very interested in the larger ship.

Avon tied up alongside the eastern jetty. She was about to be boarded by a trainload of passengers.

ORIENT LINE
CRUISES TO NORWAY & NORTHERN CAPITALS

TO NORWAY FJORDS.
CRUISE NO. 268 by s.s. " ORFORD," 20,000 TONS.

ITINERARY.			STAY HRS.
IMMINGHAM DOCK	Leave Saturday,	August 1, 6 p.m.	—
MOLDE	Arrive Monday,	August 3, 2 p.m.	4
	Leave Monday,	August 3, 6 p.m.	
TRONDHJEM	Arrive Tuesday,	August 4, 8 a.m.	10
	Leave Tuesday,	August 4, 6 p.m.	
NAES	Arrive Wednesday,	August 5, 8 a.m.	17
	Leave Thursday,	August 6, 1 a.m.	
OIE	Arrive Thursday,	August 6, 9 a.m.	1
HELLESYLT	Arrive Thursday,	August 6, 1 p.m.	1
MEROK	Arrive Thursday,	August 6, 2 p.m.	28
	Leave Friday,	August 7, 6 p.m.	
OLDEN	Arrive Saturday,	August 8, 8 a.m.	
	To land passengers for Brigsdal-brae.		
LOEN	Arrive Saturday,	August 8, 9 a.m.	13
	Leave Saturday,	August 8, 10 p.m.	
	Ship will steam up Aurlands and Naero Fjords.		
BALHOLM	Arrive Sunday,	August 9, 2 p.m.	8
	Leave Sunday,	August 9, 10 p.m.	
BERGEN	Arrive Monday,	August 10, 8 a.m.	16
	Leave Monday,	August 10, Midnight	
EIDFJORD	Arrive Tuesday,	August 11, 8 a.m.	—
	To land passengers for Haugastol, etc.		
ULVIK	Arrive Tuesday,	August 11, 9 a.m.	8
	Leave Tuesday,	August 11, 5 p.m.	
EIDFJORD	Arrive Tuesday,	August 11, 6 p.m.	—
	To pick up passengers from Haugastol, etc.		
NORHEIMSUND	Arrive Tuesday,	August 11, 9 p.m.	21
	Leave Wednesday,	August 12, 6 p.m.	
IMMINGHAM	Arrive Friday,	August 14, 7 p.m.	

This itinerary is subject to variation at the discretion of the Commander.

THIRTEEN DAYS' CRUISE.   FARE FROM 20 GNS.

ORIENT LINE
CRUISES TO NORWAY & NORTHERN CAPITALS

TO NORTHERN CAPITALS & NORWAY FJORDS.
CRUISE No. 269 by s.s. " ORONTES," 20,000 TONS.

ITINERARY.			STAY HRS.
IMMINGHAM DOCK	Leave Saturday,	August 8, 6 p.m.	—
OSLO	Arrive Monday,	August 10, 8 a.m.	10
	Leave Monday,	August 10, 6 p.m.	
STOCKHOLM	Arrive Thursday,	August 13, 10 a.m.	52
	Leave Saturday,	August 15, 2 p.m.	
HELSINGFORS	Arrive Sunday,	August 16, 8 a.m.	21
	Leave Monday,	August 17, 5 a.m.	
TALLINN	Arrive Monday,	August 17, 9 a.m.	9
	Leave Monday,	August 17, 6 p.m.	
TRAVAMUNDE	Arrive Wednesday,	August 19, 8 a.m.	10
(for Lubeck)	Leave Wednesday,	August 19, 6 p.m.	
COPENHAGEN	Arrive Thursday,	August 20, 9 a.m.	33
	Leave Friday,	August 21, 6 p.m	
	Ship will steam up Aurlands and Naero Fjords.		
BALHOLM	Arrive Sunday,	August 23, 2 p.m.	8
	Leave Sunday,	August 23, 10 p.m.	
BERGEN	Arrive Monday,	August 24, 8 a.m.	16
	Leave Monday,	August 24, Midnight	
EIDFJORD	Arrive Tuesday,	August 25, 8 a.m.	—
	To land passengers for Haugastol, etc.		
ULVIK	Arrive Tuesday,	August 25, 9 a.m.	8
	Leave Tuesday,	August 25, 5 p.m.	
EIDFJORD	Arrive Tuesday,	August 25, 6 p.m.	—
	To pick up passengers from Haugastol, etc.		
NORHEIMSUND	Arrive Tuesday,	August 25, 9 p.m.	21
	Leave Wednesday,	August 26, 6 p.m.	
IMMINGHAM*	Arrive Friday,	August 28, 7 a.m.	

This itinerary is subject to variation at the discretion of the Commander.

TWENTY DAYS' CRUISE   FARE FROM 30 GNS.

*PASSENGERS may proceed in the Steamer from IMMINGHAM to LONDON (Tilbury) on payment of 2 guineas additional, including first-class rail fare, Tilbury to St. Pancras.

Orient line cruise itineraries, possibly for the 1929 season.

ORIENT LINE

DINNER

CONSOMMÉ MADRILÈNE
POTAGE FERMIÈRE

SAUMON, SAUCE AMÉRICAINE

TÊTE DE VEAU EN TORTUE
ASPERGES AU BEURRE

Sorbet au Citron

ROAST SIRLOIN OF BEEF, YORKSHIRE PUDDING
BRAISED YORK HAM, PURÉE OF SPINACH

ROAST CAPON, SÉVIGNÉ
ROAST PTARMIGAN, BREAD SAUCE
SALAD

GOOSEBERRY TART
VANILLA BAVAROISE   CHOCOLATE NUT SUNDÆ
FRIANDISES

FOIE DE VOLAILLE SUR CROÛTE

COLD SIDEBOARD:
LEICESTER PIE   ROAST QUARTER OF LAMB

S.S. "ORFORD."   21ST JULY, 1929

LUNCHEON

BOUILLI SOUP

FRIED PLAICE

DEVONSHIRE PIE
SAVOURY TOAST

TO ORDER—MACÉDOINE OMELETTE

FROM THE GRILL (TO ORDER) 15 MINUTES
MUTTON CHOPS   RUMP STEAKS
PORK CUTLETS

POTATOES:
BOILED JACKET, FRENCH FRIED, SARATOGA.
PURÉE, LYONNAISE

COLD SIDEBOARD:
LOBSTER MAXIMILIAN
OXFORD BRAWN, OPORTO SAUCE
YORK HAM | PRESSED SPICED BEEF
LUNCHEON SAUSAGE | GALANTINE OF CHICKEN
MAYONNAISE SAUCE
ROAST SHOULDER OF LAMB, MINT JELLY

SALAD:
LETTUCE, TOMATO, BEETROOT, JAPONAISE

RICE CUSTARD
COMPÔTE OF RED CURRANTS
BOILED CURRANT ROLL

CHEESE:
CHEDDAR, CAMEMBERT, GRUYÈRE

BREADS:
PULLED, GRISINI, RYVITA, VITA-WEAT, ENERGEN

SCOTCH OATCAKE

S.S. "ORFORD."   25TH JULY, 1929

Menu cards from a 1929 cruise. These people lived in style!

ORIENT LINE

List of Passengers by

S.S. "ORFORD," 20,000 Tons.

CRUISE TO NORWEGIAN FJORDS.

Captain:
Commander A. L. OWENS, R.D., R.N.R.

Chief Officer: First Officer
C. FOX.   Lieut.-Com. J. C. K. DOWDING,
R.D., R.N.R.

Surgeon: Purser:
J. A. McILROY,   E. W. ROPE.
M.R.C.S., L.R.C.P.

Chief Engineer:
S. GRANT.

Liaison Officer:
Rear-Admiral H. M. EDWARDS, C.B., R.N.

FROM IMMINGHAM, 20th JULY, 1929.

Mr. and Mrs. H. J. ADAMS	Miss A. C. BARTLETT
Miss M. E. ADAMS	Mr. W. BENNETT
Miss O. M. ADAMS	Miss L. E. BENNETT
Mr. W. ARMITAGE	Mr. H. B. BERLINER
Miss A. ARMITAGE	Mr. and Mrs. E. D. BERRY
Miss R. A. ATKINSON	Mr. and Mrs. J. BERRY
Mr. F. L. ATTENBOROUGH	Miss I. A. BERRY
Miss N. M. ATTERTON	Mr. N. A. BERRY
Dr. T. BAILLIE	Mr. and Mrs. C. D. BISSET
Mrs. BAILLIE	Miss P. BROAD
Mr. J. BAIRSTOW	Miss J. BROADY
Mme. de BALAN	Mr. and Mrs. G. A. BROMAGE
Rev. J. H. BALMFORTH	Miss E. G. BROMAGE
Miss M. L. BARKER	Miss M. A. BROMAGE
Mr. D. BARNES	Miss E. M. BROWN
Miss C. BARNETT	Mr. C. J. BURGESS

The passenger list from the same cruise.

SS *Orontes* tied up at the eastern jetty, *c*.1931.

A shot of the *Orontes* taken on the same day. The people in the foreground are relatives of Mr Roy Porter of Leicester, formerly of Grimsby, who took the photograph. All the people in these two pictures would have held day visitor passes to look around the ship.

SS *Orion*, 23,000 tons, sister ship of the *Orontes*, from a ship's postcard.

Passengers disembark from SS *Orford* while white-coated attendants stand by the open doors of the waiting train.

The passenger's luggage follows them ashore. The coach on the right of the picture has a clerestory roof.

Passengers watch the arrival of one of the special trains, drawn by a GC locomotive, in the late 1920s.

Sometimes the cruise ships were berthed within the dock. Here SS *Avon* passes through the lock.

Locals gather near the dock offices to watch a departure.

An interesting shot of people watching a departure from within the dock. Possibly the reason for using the dock was that another liner was berthed on the eastern jetty, seen faintly in the background. A wagon belonging to the southern railway is marshalled with LNER vehicles in front of Hewson's chandlery.

SS *Arandora Star* enters the lock with attendant tug.

Private cars and taxis line up near the end of the eastern jetty to await their passengers. Private cars were stored by Mr Bacon in garages to the rear of market buildings whilst their owners cruised.

The crew of the *Arandora Star* relax between cruises.

Arandora Star inches through the locks.

A misty departure for the *Arandora Star*. This ship was torpedoed in the Atlantic on 2 July 1940, whilst carrying Axis POWs to Canada, resulting in the deaths of 740 crew, soldiers and POWs. The sinking was claimed by Gunther Prien, captain of the U47, which was responsible for the sinking of HMS *Royal Oak* at Scapa flow earlier in the war.

Seven
The Railway Scene

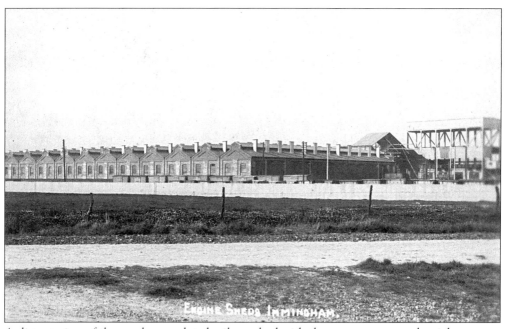

ENGINE SHEDS IMMINGHAM.

A distant view of the newly completed railway shed with the water tower on the right.

The camera moves in closer...

...and yet closer. Robinson 2-8-0S stands inside the shed – in early days, to judge by the lack of soot on the girders.

Interior view of the shed, showing the inspection pits.

A better photograph of the railcar seen on the left, above. This picture was taken at the temporary platform at Pyewipe, Grimsby, in the period before the electric trams came into operation, when a steam railcar service was provided for workmen.

A period postcard showing acres of empty sidings with the coaling hoists in the background.

This is what the sidings were intended for!

LNER class B3 4-6-0 No.6165 *Valour* leaving Immingham with a midnight sun special in 1935. *Valour* was named in honour of Great Central employees who gave their lives in the Great War. The engine was allocated intermittently to Immingham shed from 1928.

A close-up shot of *Valour*'s splasher-mounted nameplate.

Another Immingham ex-GCR 'namer', class B3 *Earl Beatty* in LNER days with a Grimsby town football special heading for a match in London.

The late Bill Botham of Immingham (left) with two of his workmates. These three young engine cleaners are standing in front of B3 *Lord Stuart of Wortley* having just prepared it for a Cleethorpes to Leicester express in the 1920s.

Three ex-GC engines standing outside Immingham shed in the 1930s. B3 *Lord Faringdon* stands in the centre, flanked by a dock tank and a J11 O-6-O.

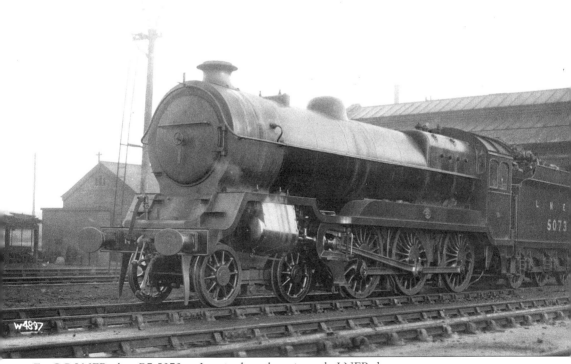

Ex-GC LNER class B7 5073 at Immingham loco in early LNER days.

Another Immingham B7 passes through Barnetby on a boat train special.

More engine cleaners! Women's war work. During the Great War, whilst the men were in khaki, many jobs were taken over (but only for the duration!) by their wives and daughters. These women are busy cleaning *Immingham* class loco No.1095 at Immingham shed, c.1915.

INGHAM (GREAT CENTRAL RAILWAY) F.C. 1914/15;

They don't look happy! Have they just lost a cup match?

Mrs Staples dressed for duty in a dock
signal box during the First World War.

Nineteenth-century technology. A double-framed Sacre 4-4-0 stands at Immingham dock station with a rake of six-wheeled carriages in GCR (pre-1923) days.

Immingham driver Dick Burnett with vital equipment!

LNER days, but the vintage coaches remain. A Pollitt 4-4-0 waits at the dock station.

A GCR station master, whose identity is unknown.

Immingham Dock Railway Station Mk 1. Built on the riverside to the west of the locks, the station handled passenger trains from New Holland via Goxhill and, in later days, worker's trains for the graving dock from Grimsby via Habrough and Ulceby. The power station can be seen in the background.

The permanent station, built on the opposite side of the track. Passenger services ended in the 1960s, although the station buildings remained until the late 1980s. The pole squatter in the upper background seemed determined to be in the picture.

The crew of a J11 Pom-Pom pose for the camera.

The Ritz Hotel of the GCR system! There was nowhere else to lodge and the dormitory was built near Kings Road Bridge to accommodate visiting train crews. The shed and water tower can be seen on the extreme left.

A dormitory interior. The main corridor shows the rooms opening off to each side.

Another interior of the dormitory. There were no great home comforts here. This was the kitchen area with cooking range prominent.

The recreation area in the dormitory. Note the portraits of GC locomotives on the walls in this and the previous photograph.

The demise of the dormitory in the 1960s. This view shows its neglected condition shortly before its demolition.

No.1097 *Immingham* again. A fine shot believed to have been taken on the day of the sod-cutting in 1906. Engine and coaches are in a sparkling condition.

A gathering of dignitaries at the sod-cutting ceremony after alighting from their train.

Robinson Atlantic at the coaling stage. The dishevelled condition of No.2923 makes identification difficult. This view is obviously taken in late LNER days, as indicated by the WD saddle tank 0-6-0 behind.

Another Robinson Atlantic outside the shed, with an O4 2-8-0 in the background.

In contrast this with the last two photographs, a 'Jersey Lily' in sparkling GCR livery.

An unidentified O4 2-8-0 coaled up and ready for duty stands outside the shed. Its driver checks round with his oilcan.

The empty sidings signal box, photographed in recent years, with the water tower behind.

Inside the box. When built, it was at the forefront of technology, being equipped with electric switches rather than traditional hand operated levers.

The enlarged signal box at Ulceby Junction, erected to handle the increased traffic generated by the dock. The staff, in a variety of uniforms, pose for the camera.

The signal box at Immingham west, controlling the entry from Ulceby Junction.

Eight

A Final Look – The War Years And After

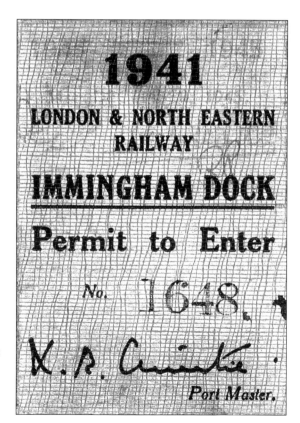

Under the defence regulations, entry to the dock estate was strictly controlled during the Second World War. All authorized persons had to carry a permit card such as this.

Because of restrictions, wartime photographs are rare. The graving dock was kept extremely busy. HMS *Fancy* and HMS *Cotswold* are shown here in dry dock in 1944.

Close-up view of an unidentified warship undergoing repairs to its bow.

Wartime food shortages prompted unorthodox farming methods. This piggery was situated near the graving dock. Note the security lock on the heavy steel gate. The last three photographs

are taken from the records of the Humber Graving Dock Company, now defunct.

IDENTIFICATION CARD.

154.

London & North Eastern Railway

The undermentioned person is authorised to be on the Lines and Premises of the London & North Eastern Railway Company while in the execution of his or her duty. This card is valid until cancelled or withdrawn.

Name *in Full* .... BOTHAM, WILLIAM JAMES.

Department .... Locomotive Running

Grade .... Fireman.

Stationed *at* .... IMMINGHAM.

Signature *of Holder* .... *W. J. Botham*

This Identification Card must be signed in ink by the holder immediately on receipt, and be carried until further notice when engaged in work on the Railway. It must be produced at any time on request, and the holder must, if required, sign his or her name as a proof of identity.

Signature of
Issuing Officer

L.N.E.R. LINCOLN
R.H.R. GALLOWAY
PER ....
DISTRICT LOCO. SUPT.

BY ORDER

Railway workers identification card issued to fireman Bill Botham.

A group of wartime naval ratings photographed in dock at Immingham.

H.M.S. KELLY,

c/o G.P.O.,

LONDON.

22nd April, 1941.

Dear Mrs. Botham,

　　　　　Commander Walker has written to tell me
of the closing down of the Royal Naval Club at
Immingham, but I feel I cannot just let it fade away
without writing to thank you for all the good work
you did to keep it going, and to make it such a
successful rendezvous for naval ratings at Immingham.

　　　　　Although it is some months since ships
of my Flotilla visited Immingham, I can assure you
that the Royal Naval Club is remembered by the men,
and that they appreciate your kindness in giving your
time and hard work to this voluntary cause.

　　　　　Yours sincerely,

Louis Mountbatten

CAPTAIN (D),
FIFTH DESTROYER FLOTILLA.

Lord Louis Mountbatten's destroyer group was based at Immingham for a period during the Second World War. Lord Louis occupied an office in the County Hotel. This self explanatory letter from His Lordship expresses regret at the passing of the local Royal Naval Club.

The Jacklin twins, local boys who signed on for naval service at Immingham dock in 1939.

Moving on in time. On 4 August 1957 HMS *Sheffield* collided with the lock wall whilst entering on an official visit. Tide and wind conditions had made for a difficult entry.

April 1962. Ford Anglia Cars stand awaiting export. The grain silo dominates the background.

May 1960. Before the erection of the riverside bulk terminal, iron ore is discharged into railway wagons at the mineral quay.

September 1967. A Pickford's heavy tractor stands awaiting its load, a seventy-two ton furnace for the Laporte factory at Stallingborough, which is being discharged using a floating crane.

Acknowledgements

Grateful thanks for permission to use photographs in this book are due to the following: Maurice Barrick; Eric Rands; Roy Barnard; Robert Mack; Mike Fish and David Jackson of the Great Central Railway Society.

North East Lincolnshire libraries; Welholme Galleries Grimsby; National Railway Museum; Real Photographs; Immingham Museum.

All royalties from this publication will be donated to the Immingham Museum.